be nice.

Salena Corner

Tahoma Publishing

be nice.

beniceonline.com

be nice. is a mental health education, bully and suicide prevention initiative that creates a positive, cultural change through simple, daily actions.

be nice. is a self-starting curriculum and kit for schools, communities, and businesses.

Learn more: beniceonline.com

Notice. Invite. Challenge. Empower.

#benice

To my amazing son, Sam, who is the kindest boy I know, who teaches me to be a better person every day, and makes my heart burst with love.

To my wonderful husband, Chris, my best friend and partner in life, the one who loves and supports me unconditionally, the calm to my storm, and the one who fills me with an indescribable love.

I love you both more than words could ever say.

Be nice to your friends.

Be nice to those you don't know.

Be nice and make sure your kindness always shows.

Be nice to those who have less.
Be nice to those who have more.

Be nice to the one
sitting alone by
the door.

Be nice because you can.

Be nice because you care.

Be nice even when there is nobody there.

Be nice to the girls.
Be nice to the boys.

Be nice even when there is so much angry noise.

Be nice when they are strangers.

Be nice when they are friends.

Be nice and make sure your niceness never ends.

Be nice to the young.
Be nice to the old.

Be nice even when you are not told.

Be nice to those who are different.

Be nice to those who are the same.

Be nice to the people who do not even know your name.

Be nice every minute.

Be nice from the start.

Be nice because you know it is right in your heart.

Be nice because it feels good
and is the right thing to do.

BE NICE...
One day you will
need someone to
be nice to you.

www.ingramcontent.com/pod-product-compliance
Lightning Source LLC
Chambersburg PA
CBHW041223040426
42443CB00002B/67